MEANINGFUL CHANGE

How Donald Trump has united a country and affected the world in a positive way

Michael Davidson

meaningful change

Copyright © 2018 Michael Davidson Studio

Printed in the United States
First Edition – July 2018

All rights reserved. No part of this publication may be produced, stored, or transmitted in any form or by any means, electronic, mechanical, photocopying, recording, or otherwise without the written prior permission of the author.

Davidson, Michael 1969 –

www.michaeldavidsonstudio.com

ISBN-10: 1719082405
ISBN-13: 978-1719082402

meaningful change

DEDICATION

To my girls...

Apologies for not leaving you a better world.

meaningful change

meaningful change

CONTENTS

Acknowledgments   *i*
Forward   *ii*

1	THE GREAT RISE TO POWER	1
2	UNITING A PARTY/UNITING A HOUSE	15
3	BORDER SECURITY/THE AMAZING WALL	29
4	IMMIGRATION	43
5	RACE RELATIONS IN AMERICA	57
6	THE INTELLIGENCE COMMUNITY	71
7	GLOBAL SYNERGY	85
8	CLIMATE CHANGE/THE ENVIRONMENT	99
9	THE INSPIRING USE OF SOCIAL MEDIA	113
10	THE INTEGRITY OF THE OFFICE	127
11	A MORAL EXAMPLE	141
	About the Author	162

meaningful change

meaningful change

ACKNOWLEDGMENTS

My thanks to Donald Trump for providing the volumes of emptiness
that will be written about for centuries

meaningful change

FORWARD

All our lives we grow up with a sense of reverence for the highest office in the world. Whether you are an American citizen or from the far-reaches of the planet, the President of the United States held a status well beyond other positions of title. It resembled many things- strength, power, influence. But never before has it created such controversy, division and uncertainty in a country and the global community as a whole. Never before has it been relegated to a punchline. I think this book says it all.

After the amusement subsides, please use these pages as your personal notebook to write how you can be the voice of change in the world. It needs it.

Michael Davidson
July 2018

meaningful change

meaningful change

meaningful change

1

THE GREAT RISE TO POWER

the great rise to power

the great rise to power

****

the great rise to power

the great rise to power

the great rise to power

the great rise to power

*** * * * * * * * * * *

the great rise to power

the great rise to power

the great rise to power

※※※※※※※※※※※

the great rise to power

the great rise to power

the great rise to power

the great rise to power

∗∗∗∗∗∗∗∗∗∗∗

2

UNITING A PARTY/UNITING A HOUSE

uniting a party/uniting a house

✦✦✦✦✦✦✦✦✦✦✦✦✦

uniting a party/uniting a house

※※※※※※※※※※※

uniting a party/uniting a house

uniting a party/uniting a house

uniting a party/uniting a house

uniting a party/uniting a house

uniting a party/uniting a house

uniting a party/uniting a house

uniting a party/uniting a house

uniting a party/uniting a house

uniting a party/uniting a house

uniting a party/uniting a house

✳✳✳✢✣✳✳✳✳✳✣✢

uniting a party/uniting a house

7

3

BORDER SECURITY/THE AMAZING WALL

border security/the amazing wall

border security/the amazing wall

※※※+※※※※※+

border security/the amazing wall

border security/the amazing wall

※※※※ * * ※※※※※※ * *

border security/the amazing wall

border security/the amazing wall

****

border security/the amazing wall

border security/the amazing wall

border security/the amazing wall

border security/the amazing wall

+++*++

border security/the amazing wall

border security/the amazing wall

border security/the amazing wall

4

IMMIGRATION

immigration

****

immigration

immigration

immigration

****

immigration

immigration

immigration

immigration

immigration

immigration

immigration

* * * * * * * * * * * *

immigration

※※※※†※※※※※※※†

immigration

+++******+++***

5

RACE RELATIONS IN AMERICA

race relations in America

race relations in America

****

race relations in America

race relations in America

race relations in America

race relations in America

✳✳✳✴✲✳✳✳✳✳✴✴

race relations in America

race relations in America

****

race relations in America

race relations in America

race relations in America

race relations in America

race relations in America

6

THE INTELLIGENCE COMMUNITY

the intelligence community

the intelligence community

the intelligence community

the intelligence community

the intelligence community

the intelligence community

the intelligence community

the intelligence community

****

the intelligence community

the intelligence community

the intelligence community

the intelligence community

the intelligence community

* * * * * * * * * * * *

7

GLOBAL SYNERGY

global synergy

global synergy

global synergy

global synergy

global synergy

global synergy

global synergy

global synergy

global synergy

global synergy

global synergy

global synergy

global synergy

8

CLIMATE CHANGE/THE ENVIRONMENT

climate change/the environment

climate change/the environment

climate change/the environment

climate change/the environment

climate change/the environment

climate change/the environment

climate change/the environment

climate change/the environment

climate change/the environment

climate change/the environment

climate change/the environment

climate change/the environment

climate change/the environment

∗∗∗∗∗∗∗∗∗∗∗

THE INSPIRING USE OF SOCIAL MEDIA

the inspiring use of social media

the inspiring use of social media

the inspiring use of social media

the inspiring use of social media

the inspiring use of social media

the inspiring use of social media

the inspiring use of social media

the inspiring use of social media

the inspiring use of social media

the inspiring use of social media

the inspiring use of social media

the inspiring use of social media

the inspiring use of social media

10
THE INTEGRITY OF THE OFFICE

the integrity of the office

✝·✧✵✶✵✶✵✝·✧✵✶

the integrity of the office

the integrity of the office

****

the integrity of the office

the integrity of the office

※※※※※※※※※※※

the integrity of the office

the integrity of the office

the integrity of the office

the integrity of the office

※※※※※※※※※

the integrity of the office

✼✼✼✼✼✼✼✼✼✼✼✼

the integrity of the office

✢✢✣✤✤✤✤✤✤✢✢✣✤✤

the integrity of the office

the integrity of the office

11

A MORAL EXAMPLE

a moral example

++>>**<<*++>**

a moral example

a moral example

a moral example

※※※※✻※※※※※※※✻

a moral example

··*·*·*·*·*·*·*·*·*·*·*

a moral example

a moral example

··*****·*·*·***

a moral example

a moral example

a moral example

a moral example

a moral example

a moral example

*⁎⁎⁎⁎⁎⁎⁎⁎⁎⁎⁎⁎

a moral example

a moral example

··*·*·*·*·*·*·*·*·*·*

a moral example

a moral example

a moral example

✻✼✻✦✜✦✼✻✻✻✻✦✜

a moral example

✦✦✦✦✦✦✦✦✦✦✦✦

a moral example

****

Missed opportunity. Chaos.

ABOUT THE AUTHOR

Michael Davidson is an artist and writer who resides near London, Ontario Canada. He has a keen interest in American politics and how it shapes the world we live in. He is clearly not a Trump supporter and it is obvious this book was written in jest to point out the writer's disappointment in the leadership qualities of Donald Trump as President of the United States.

A portion of the proceeds of this book are being donated to the support environmental efforts in North America.

Made in the USA
Columbia, SC
14 November 2018